Dedication

Melanie Reed

Thank you for believing in me.
You were the first to encourage this journey.

THIS JOURNAL BELONGS TO:

IF WE'RE GOING TO MAKE
IT EVEN ONE DAY IN THIS
LIFE, THEN WE'VE GOT TO
HAVE GOD'S HELP EVERY
STEP OF THE WAY.

*He's our
need meeter, our
way maker and
our heart saver.*

MITZI NEELY

She is clothed
with strength
and dignity

AND SHE LAUGHS
WITHOUT FEAR
OF THE FUTURE.

PROVERBS 31:25 NLT

WHEN WE PUT OUR
ARMOR ON, WE MUST
BATHE EVERYTHING
IN PRAYER.

Prayer brings
us into
fellowship with God
so that His armor
protects us.

MITZI NEELY

WHEN YOU FIND YOURSELF
FEELING WEAK,
OVERWHELMED,
DISCOURAGED OR TEMPTED
BY SOMETHING OR SOMEONE,
QUICKLY PUT ON THE
ARMOR OF GOD.

Every time you do this, you're "Getting Your Jesus On".

MITZI NEELY

TRUTH, RIGHTEOUSNESS,
PEACE, FAITH AND SALVATION
ARE MORE THAN WORDS.
LEARN HOW TO APPLY THEM.
YOU'LL NEED THEM
THROUGHOUT YOUR LIFE.

*God's Word
is an
indispensable
weapon,*

EPHESIANS 6:17 MSG

Additional Resources from *Peacefully Imperfect Ministries*

Devotional Books
Dwell in the Psalms
A Thankful Heart: 30 Days to the Grateful Life

A Thankful Heart: 30 Days to the Grateful Life Bonus Kit
Scripture Reading Plan ~ Scripture Cards
Illustration Printables
30 Day Thankful Heart Challenge Journal

Nourish the Soul
30 Day Scripture Reading Plans and
Encouragement / Prayer calendars
Unshakeable Love   ~ Spiritual Growth
Declutter the Soul ~ Hope for the Soul
Criticism and Challenges ~ Joy-Filled Life
Relax, Refresh, Replenish ~ Anxiety and Fear

Eight Truths About Happiness Mini-Bible Study

20 Ways to Beat the Blues Study Packet
Scripture Reading Plan ~ 20 Ways to Beat the Blues
Scripture Cards

For more information visit: PeacefullyImperfect.net

Get Your Jesus On—Lined Journal

Copyright © 2019 by Peacefully Imperfect Ministries
All rights reserved.

www.PeacefullyImperfect.net

ISBN: 978-1796211078
Imprint: Independently published

Cover Art by: Lauren Gaskill
Cover Design by: Jana Kennedy-Spicer
Interior Design by: Jana Kennedy-Spicer

Unless noted otherwise, all scriptures are taken from the HOLY BIBLE, NEW LIVING TRANSLA-TION (NLT): Scriptures taken from the HOLY BIBLE, NEW LIVING TRANSLATION, Copyright© 1996, 2004, 2007 by Tyndale House Foundation. Used by permission of Tyndale House Publishers, Inc., Carol Stream, Illinois 60188. All rights reserved. Used by permission.

37969024R00066

Made in the USA
Middletown, DE
09 March 2019